WHAT'S SO FUNNY?

MAKING SENSE OF HUMOR

by DONNA M. JACKSON

illustrated by TED STEARN

VIKING

An imprint of Penguin Group (USA) Inc.

VIKING

Published by Penguin Group

Penguin Young Readers Group, 345 Hudson Street, New York, New York 10014, U.S.A.

Penguin Group (Canada), 90 Eglinton Avenue East, Suite 700, Toronto, Ontario, Canada M4P 2Y3
(a division of Pearson Penguin Canada Inc.)

Penguin Books Ltd, 80 Strand, London WC2R 0RL, England

Penguin Ireland, 25 St Stephen's Green, Dublin 2, Ireland (a division of Penguin Books Ltd)

Penguin Group (Australia), 250 Camberwell Road, Camberwell, Victoria 3124, Australia
(a division of Pearson Australia Group Pty Ltd)

Penguin Books India Pvt Ltd, 11 Community Centre, Panchsheel Park, New Delhi – 110 017, India

Penguin Group (NZ), 67 Apollo Drive, Rosedale, North Shore 0632, New Zealand (a division of Pearson New Zealand Ltd.)

Penguin Books (South Africa) (Pty) Ltd, 24 Sturdee Avenue, Rosebank, Johannesburg 2196, South Africa

Penguin Books Ltd, Registered Offices: 80 Strand, London WC2R 0RL, England

First published in 2011 by Viking, a division of Penguin Young Readers Group

1   3   5   7   9   10   8   6   4   2

Text copyright © Donna M. Jackson, 2011
Illustrations copyright © Ted Stearn, 2011
All rights reserved

LIBRARY OF CONGRESS CATALOGING-IN-PUBLICATION DATA
Jackson, Donna M., date–
What's so funny?: making sense of humor / by Donna M. Jackson ;
illustrated by Ted Stearn.—1st ed.
p. cm.
ISBN 978-0-670-01244-2 (hardcover)
1. Wit and humor—Psychological aspects—Juvenile literature. I. Title.
BF575.L3J23 2011   152.4'3—dc22   2010041042

Manufactured in China
Set in Berling Roman
Book design by Nancy Brennan

✿ ✿ ✿

Humor is mankind's greatest blessing.

—Mark Twain, American author and humorist (1835–1910)

✿ ✿ ✿

CONTENTS

WITH LOVE to my good-natured aunts and uncles,
and to dearest Barb, a joyful, giving spirit —D.J.

✵ ✵ ✵

ACKNOWLEDGMENTS

A WARM NOTE of thanks to all the humor experts who contributed to this fun project: Rod A. Martin, PhD, psychologist and author at the University of Western Ontario; Jaak Panksepp, PhD, neuroscientist and Baily Endowed Chair of Animal Well-Being Science at Washington State University; Steven M. Sultanoff, PhD, mirthologist and clinical psychologist; Jessica Milner Davis, PhD, honorary associate, School of Media, Arts and Letters, University of Sydney, Australia; Robert Thompson, director of the Center for the Study of Popular Television at Syracuse University; Richard Wiseman, PhD, author and psychology professor at the University of Hertfordshire, United Kingdom; John Black, owner, Pun of the Day Web site; Yakov Smirnoff, comedian, artist, psychologist; Jami Gong, comedian and founder of the TakeOut Comedy Club in Hong Kong; Judy Carter, comedian, author, and comedy coach; JoAnne Bachorowski, PhD, associate professor of psychology at Vanderbilt University; Jeff Gandy, Youth and Education programs manager, Second City Training Center, Chicago; Mark Gonzalez, comedian; Darren LaCroix, keynote speaker, comedian; Wali Collins, actor and comedian; Paul Kim, comedian and founder of the Asian talent show Kollaboration; Paul E. McGhee, humor researcher, author, and speaker; Cathy Strange; and Joni Wilson.

I'm especially grateful to the outstanding editorial team at Viking for their enthusiastic support of this book: publisher Regina Hayes, my editor extraordinaire Catherine Frank, copy editor Janet Pascal, and designer Nancy Brennan; to Ted Stearn for his humorous illustrations; to Susan Cohen and Brianne Johnson at Writers House for their guidance and expertise; and to Charlie Jackson, for a lifetime of love and laughs.

WHAT'S SOOOOOO FUNNY?

A PIE IN the face.

A slip of the tongue.

A *burrrrp* at the dinner table.

Humor. We all know it when we see it—and when we hear it. But people have defined it differently for centuries. One reason is because humor varies from person to person, and depends on factors such as age, culture, and even sex. What's funny to a two-year-old is different from what's funny to a ten-year-old or a twenty-year-old. What's funny in Western cultures differs from what's funny in Eastern cultures. What's funny to a boy is not always funny to a girl.

Humor is highly personal. Much like beauty, it's in the heart and mind of the beholder. "We're all born with a sense of humor," says Dr. William Fry, a psychiatrist and pioneer in humor studies. But it develops differently for everyone, based in part on life experiences.

"It's like a psychological fingerprint," he says—one that evolves and changes over time.

Humor is a "moment of discovery," a playful new way of looking at things. Each time you hear something funny, your brain makes new

connections, says Fry. Humor has also been described as the thrill of *getting it*—as in understanding a joke or funny situation—and *getting away with it*—as in successfully pulling a prank on a favorite cousin. It can come from witnessing the absurd, like your neighbor dancing with her cat; or breaking social rules, like giggling at a funeral. Most often, it's the pairing of two ideas, thoughts, pictures, or situations that don't quite belong together but that fit in a "nonserious," surprising way. You know, like the Florida principal who dressed in a hot-dog suit and let students spray her with ketchup and onions. Now that's funny!

Humor can make you laugh out loud—sparking a physical response that communicates your happiness to others. But you don't have to be noisy to experience humor, say experts such as psychologist Rod Martin at the University of Western Ontario. Take the principal in the hot-dog bun. Instead of laughing out loud when you read about her, you may have smiled to yourself and felt joy bubble up inside of you. Humor specialists call this feeling mirth and say it's our emotional reaction to humor—which may or may not be expressed through laughter.

Mirth is an involuntary, automatic response, says Martin, who has written a book called *The Psychology of Humor*. Much as anger is triggered when we perceive that someone is trying to intentionally wrong us, mirth arises when the thinking parts of our brain notice that something's funny and playfully out of whack. The happy feelings can range from mild amusement to absolute joy.

Mirth not only makes us feel good, it replaces distressing emotions, says psychologist Steven Sultanoff. "When you experience humor, you can't be angry, worried, or sad at the same time."

Humor changes our focus, he says.

Have you ever argued with a friend who suddenly did something funny to lighten the mood? What happened next? Did you start laughing and feel a little better? Or did you find yourself telling them to stop so that you could stay mad a little longer? "Humor tends to reduce or remove anger so we can get over the distressing feelings," explains Sultanoff.

Humor can even make serious events seem a little funnier with time. A few weeks after Hurricane Katrina devastated New Orleans in 2005, some people placed signs outside of their homes that said things like GONE WITH THE WIND and HOUSE FOR SALE—SOME ASSEMBLY REQUIRED. This showed that home owners were moving forward and coping with the disaster in a positive way, says Sultanoff. It's also a great reminder that "it's not situations that generate our stress, it's the meaning we place on the situations."

Not only does humor make us feel good, it connects us to others. That's because most types of humor involve people in some way, notes Martin. "Sometimes we'll laugh at, say, a dog that's doing something funny. But often, what's going on is that the dog reminds us of a person. . . . It's doing something humanlike that makes us laugh." The same goes for cartoon characters—we laugh because they have human traits.

Humor is a form of communication, says Martin. We often use it to say things indirectly. For example, he says some humorous greeting cards read the opposite of what they mean: *I wish I had a nickel for every time I thought of you. . . . I'd buy a stick of gum.* What the card is really communicating in a roundabout way is "I like you."

Humor also helps us communicate norms and expectations, says Martin. "Dude—take a shower!" for instance, is a funny way to tell someone, "You don't smell so good right now." When offered in a friendly tone, it makes a point without hurting the other person's feelings. Likewise, humor allows us to share information about ourselves that might be uncomfortable, such as, "I'm so afraid of heights, I get dizzy standing on my toes!" When you say something in a funny way, you can always retract it depending on how the other person reacts, he says. You can quickly add, "Only joking," or "Just kidding."

No doubt, humor is one of the important ways we get along. "It probably evolved out of our social nature," explains Martin. "We live in relationships with other people, and we need other people to survive."

Theoretically Speaking

What makes something funny?

No one knows for certain, since no one-size-fits-all answer exists. But deep thinkers, from poets to philosophers, have come up with plenty of theories. One of the earliest is the *superiority theory*—the idea that we laugh at other people's mistakes and misfortunes so that we can feel better about ourselves. This theory is based on the belief that seeing other people's faults can make us feel superior to them—whether they trip on their words or over their feet. "The superiority theory also explains why we laugh at certain types of jokes," says psychologist and author Richard Wiseman, who teamed with the British Association for the Advancement of Science in 2001 to find the world's funniest joke. (Sorry, we can't print the winner here, but it *did* fall into this category.) Many jokes create a sense of superiority by making people look silly when they do things such as misunderstand obvious situations, he says. Entries from among the more than 40,000 submitted to Wiseman's LaughLab include:

HA HA HA HA

Did you hear about the man who was proud when he completed a jigsaw puzzle within thirty minutes, because it said "5-6 years" on the box?

Some cultures even set aside a time—for instance, April Fools'
Day—for people to play tricks on one another. On April 1, 1957, a
well-respected news program in England broadcast a story highlighting
the harvest of the spaghetti crop in Switzerland. The report showed
people plucking strands of spaghetti from tree branches and then lay-
ing them out in the sun to dry. Hundreds of people were fooled by the
story, say British news officials. Many called to find out "where they
could get hold of a spaghetti bush so they could grow their own crop."
The Museum of Hoaxes in San Diego, California, calls this the top
April Fools' Day trick of all time.

Another set of theories focuses on humor as a form of mental *relief*.
Psychologist Sigmund Freud believed that humor gives us a socially
acceptable way to talk about "forbidden" thoughts and to poke fun
at scary topics such as death. (Humor about death is referred to as

What's Soooooo Funny?

"black" or "gallows" humor.) In Freud's view, the relief that we feel when expressing ideas that are uncomfortable and taboo in everyday conversations results in joyful bursts of energy called laughter.

The doctor gives a patient a check-up and looks very concerned.
Patient: OK, Doc, break it to me, how long do I have to live?
Doctor: Ten.
Patient: Ten what? Years? Months?
Doctor: . . . nine . . . eight . . . seven . . . six . . .

An alternative relief theory suggests that humor occurs when tension builds over a situation and the experience turns out to be less serious than originally thought. The relief we feel when the emotional strain is lifted triggers a smile or a laugh. For example, if someone walks into a door and his nose starts bleeding because he's broken it—that's not so funny. On the other hand, if someone walks into a door and immediately yells *yipes!* while shaking his head with embarrassment, then we're more apt to laugh. That's because we've determined that the situation is not serious and that "no real harm has been done," says brain scientist V. S. Ramachandran.

A third theory of humor, and one of the most popular, is the *incongruity theory*: the idea that humor happens when we expect one thing and get another that tickles us. *A hockey player who dances ballet. A neat freak who is best friends with a slob. An advertisement that tells us we can buy "6 donuts for $2.99—Limit 3."* The mismatched pairs can be surprising, odd, or unusual in words, pictures, experiences, or actions. Comedians often apply this theory when telling jokes— leading audiences down one path of possibilities, and abruptly changing directions at the punch line with a surprising, funny twist.

A man's at home reading a book when he hears a soft knock on the door.

He opens the door and sees a snail selling vacuum cleaners.

"Hey buddy, you want to buy a vacuum cleaner?"

"Get out of here!" yells the man, throwing the snail across the lawn.

Four years later, the man's reading another book when he hears a soft knock on the door.

What's Soooooo Funny?

He opens the door and sees that same snail.

Angry and out of breath, the snail says: "OK, pal . . . what's your problem??!!"

❂ Giggle Guide ❂

Humor can be found almost everywhere, and it comes packaged in a variety of funny forms. Which of these have you giggled at lately?

Blooper: a funny mistake, such as a news anchor flubbing a line

Comic strip: a series of drawings that together tell a humorous story

Daffy definition: an amusing word description, such as "Pasteurize—too far to see"

Improvisation: a skit created on the spot without a script

One-liner: a short joke or clever remark

Parody: a funny version of a well-known work such as a song or play

Pun: a fun play on words that sound alike or similar but have different meanings. For example, "Thanks for the brake" on a construction sign.

Situation comedy (sitcom): entertainment, seen especially on television, where characters face unusual situations that they try to resolve in funny ways

Slapstick: an exaggerated form of physical comedy, such as pie-throwing and slipping on banana peels

DIFFERENT STROKES

I wonder how much deeper the ocean would be
without sponges. —*bumper sticker*

HAVE YOU EVER laughed at a joke that no one else found funny? Or *not* laughed at a story that everyone else thought was hilarious?

It happens now and then—and for good reason. While we all live in the same funny world, each of us experiences it uniquely. When we hear a joke, we respond to it based on the way we see the world at the moment—called our perceptions—and this view is influenced by everything from our personalities to family backgrounds. The more similar two people's perceptions, the more likely they are to react to a situation or joke in the same way.

Differing views of the world play a large role in why boys and girls sometimes laugh at different things. Boys, for example, generally laugh more at physical humor, says Sultanoff. "They laugh loudest when someone slips and falls or is the butt of the joke." Body humor is also a big hit—anything that involves boogers, burping, farting, and the like.

Girls tend to laugh more at bonding humor, he says—humor that brings them closer together. With friends, they'll often say funny things to communicate their support and affection. "When somebody slips and falls, most girls' first reaction is to be empathic—and when you're empathic, you don't see the situation as funny," Sultanoff says.

But while girls can be more empathic at times, they can be equally unkind—especially when they use humor to snub or bully outsiders to their group. Often they'll tease other girls about their appearance (how big or small they are and the way they dress), academic skills (too smart or not smart enough), and physical abilities—or lack thereof—in sports or on the playground. Many times, they'll share nasty comments behind a person's back as a way to bond with each other and to keep their status in a group, says Sultanoff, adding that boys tend to aim their put-downs directly at their target. These trends appear to continue into adulthood. Research shows that while men often engage in humor "for the purpose of impressing others," women frequently use it for "group solidarity."

Whether it's boys or girls who are teasing, however, one of the best ways to respond—at least according to kids ages eight to eleven—is to use humor. When shown videotapes of a child who ignores taunts, becomes angry, or counters them with humor, kids rated the humorous response as the most effective, and the angry reaction as the least effective. Researchers also found that both the person being teased and the teaser were viewed more positively when a child used a funny comeback. Experts think that humor may help to diffuse the situation and potentially turn it into a positive one.

Age also influences what we find funny.

"Humor is basically a form of intellectual play—play with ideas," says psychologist Paul McGhee. As we grow and develop, our sense of humor reflects our new understanding of the world.

Preschoolers, for instance, find humor in misnaming people and things. They'll giggle as they point to Mommy and say "Daddy." They'll call an apple a banana and describe their fingers as their toes. "It's hilarious to call something a name you know is wrong," says McGhee. They also delight in rhyming sounds—such as *yummy, tummy, mummy*—and in putting words together in nonsense ways. As children near elementary school age, they laugh at pictures and sounds that are distorted and out of sync—such as a school bus that flies, a pig with giant ears, or a lion that squeaks like a mouse. "Potty" humor also gets the giggles going.

By about six or seven, "riddle disease" sets in, says McGhee. Children at this stage love to tell riddles over and over. Now that they know that words can have two or more meanings—and they can switch between those meanings in their mind—they love playing tricks with the language, he notes. That's what makes riddles and puns so exciting. Kids feel smart when they meaningfully link two pieces of information that seem to be unrelated.

 Did you hear about the man whose whole left side was cut off? He's all right now.

Different Strokes

With each year that passes, people's thinking becomes more sophisticated and their sense of humor expands. One study, noted by Rod Martin in his humor book, showed that students in grades two through seven typically preferred riddles based on language play: *"Why do birds fly south? It's too far to walk."* By tenth grade, they preferred more absurd riddles, such as, *"How can you fit six elephants into a Volkswagen Beetle? Three in the front and three in the back."*

Most day-to-day humor doesn't come packaged in jokes and riddles, however. It happens spontaneously as we interact with family and friends. We make funny comments and do funny things. We also make light of situations using more subtle forms of humor, such as irony—where you say one thing and mean something very different. Someone might say, for instance, "Wonderful weather . . ."  when they *really* mean it's rainy and miserable (and we have to stay inside!).

Studies show that while children begin to understand subtle types of humor at around eight or nine, their appreciation of it continues to grow stronger through their teens and early twenties. One reason is because these kinds of humor are complex and require knowledge on many levels. Not only do listeners need to understand *what's* being said and the implied meaning, they also need to understand its social context—*how* it's being communicated (in what tone of voice) and whether the speaker's intentions are positive or negative.

Global Appeal

Along with individual differences, culture greatly affects how we appreciate and use humor. It also influences what subjects are considered appropriate and "laughable." Americans, for instance, typically enjoy jokes about topics in the news and wordplay such as puns. Like many people around the world, they laugh at humorous stories about family and physical comedy along the lines of comedian Jim Carrey's. They also like to poke fun at politicians—a right not all citizens of every country can freely exert. In some places, people have been jailed or even killed for making fun of government officials.

No matter what the topic, the British tend to prefer their humor dry and clever. "In Britain and Australia, we use a lot of straight-faced humor," says Jessica Milner Davis of the Australasian Humor Studies Network at the University of Sydney. "Not everyone uses this form," she says, "so it doesn't always translate well across cultures."

People surveyed from European countries such as France, Denmark, and Belgium say they favor jokes that are a bit surreal or absurd, including the following from Wiseman's LaughLab experiment.

An Alsatian dog went to a telegram office, took out a blank form, and wrote: "Woof. Woof. Woof. Woof. Woof. Woof. Woof. Woof. Woof."

Different Strokes

The clerk examined the paper and politely told the dog, "There are only nine words here. You could send another 'Woof' for the same price."

"But," the dog replied, "that would make no sense at all."

In Japan, you must have *warai no ba*—an appropriate container of time—for using humor, notes Davis. "It's a time and a place where laughter is permitted and expected."

During business hours, for example, Japanese people are typically serious and hardworking. But after hours, you'll find many watching games on TV such as "human bowling" (with helmets) or "binocular soccer," where players fumble around the field essentially wearing giant magnifying glasses that distort their vision.

Chinese audiences generally prefer long, well-told jokes and funny stories. So says comedian Jami Gong, founder of the TakeOut Comedy Club in Hong Kong—the first full-time comedy club in Asia. They also respond with quiet laughs and giggles. "Local Chinese people are not used to laughing out loud in public next to strangers," says Gong. "They tend to cover their mouths and laugh on the inside." Once when a Chinese woman "laughed like crazy" during a show, her friend turned around and shushed her!

"It's a cultural thing," says Gong, but one that's changing with time.

History of the Ha Ha Ha's

Humor hasn't always been thought of as funny—particularly in Western cultures. Before the sixteenth century, it wasn't even linked with laughter, which, as it turns out, also wasn't always associated with a merry meaning. While we may all be born with a sense of humor, history shows that how we define it depends greatly on the attitudes and values of the people around us.

From the time of ancient Greece through the Middle Ages, the word "humor" referred to body fluids. Back then, doctors believed the body was made of four important, but gross, humors—blood, phlegm (mucus), yellow bile, and black bile—and they used these to identify and treat illnesses. Healthy people had the proper balance of fluids; sick people did not. The four humors also became markers of personality traits and moods. Cheerful people, for example, were considered to be rich in blood. (You wouldn't want to be diagnosed with too much blood, however. That might result in a "cure" of bloodletting!)

By the 1500s, the link between humors and being "unbalanced" eventually led to the word's use for any abnormal behavior, says humor expert Rod Martin. "Thus, a 'humor' came to mean an odd, eccentric, or peculiar person"—someone who was often laughed at and ridiculed.

This fit with laughter's mostly negative meaning at the time. "No distinction was made between 'laughing with' and 'laughing at,' since all laughter was thought to arise from making fun of someone," says Martin. Common targets included people with mental illnesses and physical deformities, such as hunchbacks.

Fast-forward a few hundred years. Now people generally saw laughter more as a "response to cleverness" in conversations, rather than as contempt. Society also began to view snickering at the less fortunate as rude and unrefined. This was in keeping with its new emphasis on compassion toward others.

Before long, a distinction began to be made between laughter originating from friendly intentions—now referred to as *humor*—and laughter arising from unfriendly, clever aims—called *wit*. "Not surprisingly, humor came to be seen as more socially desirable than wit," explains

Martin, and by the twentieth century, it evolved into a catchall term for *all* sources of laughter.

Still, some people continued to frown on laughter of all types. "As recently as the 1860s, it was considered impolite to laugh in public in the United States," notes Martin. Even in the early 1900s it was considered inappropriate to engage in humor or laughter in religious and educational places.

Today humor's encouraged almost everywhere and covers a wide range of comical territory, from lighthearted clowning to mean-spirited roasts. Most times, it is viewed (much like laughter) as positive, healthy, and socially appealing—but, as in the past, humor can still pack a bite. It depends largely on who's delivering the punch line and how it's being received.

✿ Got Gelos? ✿

Gelos: Greek for laughter

Gelotology: the study of humor and laughter and how it affects the mind and body

Gelotologist: a scientist who studies the effects of humor and laughter

Gelotherapy: a method of treating people's illnesses by helping them to laugh

HUMOR STYLES

I told you I was sick.

—*epitaph on a gravestone in Key West, Florida*

HOW WE USE humor tells the world a lot about us and how we relate to others, says psychologist Rod Martin. Positive humor can build friendships and help us handle life's challenges, while negative humor can hurt people and relationships. Martin has identified four main types of humor that people use in everyday communications. Two are generally positive and helpful—*bonding* and *laugh-at-life humor*—and two are typically negative and hurtful—*put-down* and *laugh-at-me humor*. All forms are funny, he says. But if used regularly, negative styles of humor can chip away at your self-image and leave you lonely.

- - -

Bonding humor connects people through positive feelings and is usually friendly and playful. People who use this type of humor say funny things and tell amusing stories to entertain friends, build relationships, and ease tensions. They enjoy making others laugh in a way that feels good to themselves and those around them. If they tease, it tends to communicate friendship and affection.

"I was a funny kid, and enjoyed making my parents laugh," says Yakov Smirnoff, an American comedian who spent the first part of his life in Soviet Russia. "Growing up, we had nine families living in one apartment. Each family occupied one room—one family lived in the den, another in the living room, etc. So when my parents wanted to be romantic, they would send me to look out the window.

"My dad would say: 'So what do you see out the window?'

"And I'd say: 'Our neighbors being romantic.'

"Then he'd say: 'How can you tell?'

"And I'd say: 'Because their son is looking at me.'"

When Yakov's parents laughed at his joke, he felt "'the presence of love.' I put those two things together in my mind—that love and laughter are inseparable, and that inspired me to continue to make people laugh," he says.

- - -

Humor Styles

Laugh-at-life (or *self-enhancing*) *humor* is coping humor, says Martin. It's looking at the funny side of not-so-funny things that happen to us. When a friend leans over in class and says, "Just what I was hoping for, a surprise math quiz!" he's using laugh-at-life humor to convey his fear and face it with a smile. This is one of the functions of humor, says Martin—to lessen the importance of some situations, so they don't seem so threatening. It gives  us a sense of mastery and control, while at the same time reminding us not to take ourselves—or the world—too seriously.

But humor also has a dark side. While it often brings people together, it can be used to exclude outsiders, says Martin. Some people, for example, use humor to unite against those who may act differently, dress differently, or believe differently from them.

One way they do this is by using *put-down humor*—humor that's aggressive and includes unfriendly teasing, mocking, and sarcasm—a type of praise that's really meant to insult. (*Nice job, Einstein!*) Comedians often use this type of humor to poke fun at celebrities and politicians, but it's especially hurtful if it's personal. When classmates embarrass and make fun of others, they're often trying to use put-down humor to increase their status with friends. It may work temporarily, but ultimately it creates pain and turns people off.

Laugh-at-me humor is put-down humor that people point at themselves. While laughing at our flaws can be healthy in small doses, a few people take this form of humor to extremes. They may feel insecure and offer themselves as targets so that others will like them. Some class clowns fall into this category—gaining attention by constantly goofing off and allowing others to make fun of them. Warning: Too much of this style of humor can be bad for your health and leave you depressed!

✹ It Could Be Worse . . . ✹

Humor helps us deal more successfully with uncomfortable situations, says clinical psychologist Steve Sultanoff. Let's say you're nervous about reading a story in front of the class. One way to deal with your butterflies is to use "exaggeration humor," he says. Tell yourself: It could be worse if . . . I had to sing in front of everyone or do a chicken dance for the principal. The crazier the scenarios, the more you shrink the problem down to size.

LAUGHING MATTERS

When a Navajo baby laughs for the first time, the community celebrates. Laughter signals that the child is ready to engage the world. The person who inspires the first giggle also rejoices and "hosts an *A'wee Chi'deedloh* ('The Baby Laughed') ceremony." It's believed the baby will assume his or her personality traits.

LAUGHTER. IT'S ONE language we all speak—no matter where we live or what our age. Babies typically laugh by the time they're four months old. In fact, after crying, laughing is one of the first sounds they make. Even infants who are born blind and deaf laugh. This suggests that laughter is not something we learn, but an instinctive part of our human nature.

Early on, babies laugh mostly at physical humor, such as funny faces, lip-popping, and raspberries on the belly. Many believe these playful exchanges strengthen the bonds between infants and their families. By about one year, babies begin to understand more regarding what's normal and not-so-normal behavior—especially for their parents and those around them. As a result, they'll laugh when they see the silly and unexpected, such as their older brothers and sisters quacking like ducks.

"Laughter's about relationships," says Robert Provine, assistant director of neuroscience at the University of Maryland in Baltimore County. It's a mysterious "hidden language" that's mostly meant to connect people together like social glue. It's also "one of our most honest signals," he says, and is difficult to fake. Laughter happens spontaneously—and not just when someone tells a joke.

Provine knows this because he spent ten years studying laughter in everyday situations—in malls, at zoos, and along city streets. After recording more than two thousand instances of laughter, he found that in about 85 percent of the cases, laughs followed ordinary comments.

People laughed after statements such as "I'll see you guys later," *ha ha ha* . . . "Do you have a rubber band?" *ha ha ha*. Remarkably, the laughs punctuated the ends of sentences—like periods or exclamation points. Provine also found that laughter is thirty times more likely to happen in social situations than when we're alone, say, watching TV or listening to the radio. Overall, he says, the results indicated that people—not jokes—are what's most important in sparking laughs. Laughing, in general, seems to be a playful way to tell others that we like and agree with them.

😎 Viral messages

Sometimes laughter can be catching. Just hearing someone laugh can get us giggling. Take the strange case of contagious laughter that broke out in a rural village of Tanganyika (now called Tanzania), Africa. On January 30, 1962, several middle-school girls suddenly started laughing in class. The fits of laughter quickly spread to the rest of the group, then the whole school, and eventually to nearby villages. A medical journal article from 1963 describes the laughing jags:

> *The incubation period is from a few hours to a few days. The onset is sudden, with attacks of laughing and crying lasting for a few minutes to a few hours, followed by a respite and then a recurrence. . . .*

During the six months that followed, schools closed, and hundreds of people in the community were struck by the epidemic, including boys, girls, and some adults. While the case is unusual and extreme, it demonstrates the infectious power of laughter, says Provine—something we've all experienced.

It doesn't seem to matter whether the laughs are real or not. In one experiment, Provine played recorded laughs to people, and it set them laughing for no reason in particular. In another study, researchers in England found that people's brains react and they tend to smile when they hear others laugh. The scientists believe the smiling could be a "mirroring" or mimicking effect that helps people bond together in groups.

What makes laughter so irresistible?

It's possible that we have a kind of "auditory laugh detector—a neural circuit in the brain that responds exclusively to laughter," says Provine. "Once triggered, the laugh detector activates a laugh generator, a neural circuit that causes us in turn to produce laughter."

One team of doctors may have tapped into that circuit while operating on a sixteen-year-old epilepsy patient named A.K. During

surgery, the doctors stimulated parts of the girl's brain with electricity to map its surface and pinpoint the functions of each region.

While charting the brain, surgeons stimulated a small area that's associated with complex motor movements, and A.K. burst into laughter. It didn't matter what she was looking at—a picture of a horse or people in the room—everything seemed funny to her when the region was stimulated, say doctors. Low currents generated a smile, and high currents caused "a robust contagious laughter."

Why would an area of the brain linked to motor movements cause laughter?

Researchers believe the region is probably part of a larger network that coordinates all the important ingredients of humor: the thinking parts of "getting it," the good feelings of mirth, and the muscle movements of smiling and laughter.

All in Your Head

Humor is serious stuff. Just ask brain scientists. Using images of the brain, they're helping to pinpoint what exactly happens when we find something funny. What they've found is that humor activates many areas of the brain. This includes the language comprehension centers, which help us understand funny jokes and expressions, and the emotional rewards regions, which release chemicals in the body that make us feel good. One study found that the funnier the joke, the more activity in the emotional reward centers, which indicates the subjects were feeling greater pleasure.

Researchers have also discovered that men and women process humor a little differently. Brain scans show that women use more of the brain's problem-solving areas than men when initially deciding whether something's funny. As a result, women take a little longer to make up their minds about what's humorous. When they do find something funny, however, the data suggests they feel a deeper sense of joy.

One study has even found that the subject of a joke—whether it's politics or the family—may be less important than the *way* we solve the comic problem in our brains. "The logic by which the incongruity is resolved matters most, in terms of what kind of person a joke appeals to," says Andrea Samson at the University of Fribourg in Switzerland. After showing volunteers a series of cartoons, Samson found that most people's brains became more active when they looked at comics with straightforward punch lines than when they looked at ones with "nonsense" or surreal punch lines—those that left questions to the imagination. A few people with what scientists call "experience-seeking" personalities, however, responded more strongly to the nonsense cartoons. Samson believes this may be because experience seekers thrive on novelty, and absurd jokes allow the mind to explore more possibilities than quickly resolved humor.

"Getting a joke [and laughing] would seem—on the surface—to be a very trivial, intuitive process," says Samson. "But brain imaging is showing us that there is more going on than we might think."

ANATOMY OF A LAUGH

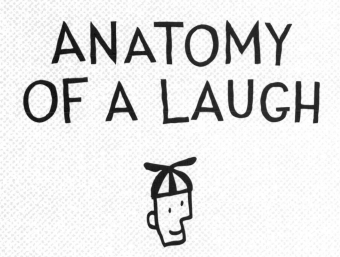

LAUGHING CAN BE a regular workout. Some call it "internal jogging." Along with bending and stretching your funny bone, it exercises your brain and flexes more than a hundred muscles from your face to your feet—especially if you really yuk it up. Follow what happens in the life of a laugh:

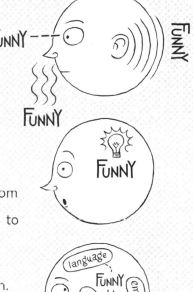

- ✖ You see, hear, feel, read, or smell something funny.

- ✖ Your brain interprets it—collecting information from regions specializing in everything from language to emotions to memories.

- ✖ You smile, turning up the corners of your mouth. Your head rolls back, your eyes narrow . . .

before you know it, you start to snicker. Experts say holding back a snicker can build gas. . . . No need to worry about that—the snicker evolves into a giggle, which rolls into laughter.

❄ By now you're breathing more heavily, your heart is beating faster, and the muscles in your chest, thorax, diaphragm, and stomach are tightening and releasing.

❄ Strange sounds erupt from your mouth and nose. *Ha, ha, ha, ha . . . hee, hee, hee, haw. Snort, snort . . . sniffle, sniffle . . . hoot, hoot . . . holler, holler . . . GRUNT.*

❄ Your friend sees you and cracks up. Only he's a silent laugher, holding it all in until telltale gasps for air give him away. Oh no . . . the rest of your friends are getting into the act, doubling up with laughter.

❄ You rock back and forth, stomp your feet, and fall out of your chair. Tears stream down your face, and your muscles start to ache. You're totally out of control. This is what they mean when they say something is "side-splittingly funny."

When you've finished laughing, a wave of relaxation washes over you. You've worked out your respiratory, muscular, and cardiovascular systems. You've lifted your mood, boosted your thinking skills, and increased your energy. You're also looking more attractive to those around you. Not only are your eyes sparkling, but you've shared a warm, friendly side of yourself that connects with others. Not a bad way to burn a few calories.

MORE ATTRACTIVE

GOOD MOOD

INCREASED ENERGY

BOOSTED THINKING SKILLS

Relaxation

✖ Funny Bone? ✖

Sticks and stones may break your bones, but not your funny bone. Turns out, it isn't really a bone—or especially funny. It's a major nerve, called the ulnar nerve, which weaves its way through the muscles and tissues of the neck all the way to the hand. When people hit their elbow on just the right spot— the area where this nerve is particularly close to the skin—it creates a numbing, pins-and-needles sensation that travels down to the pinky and part of the ring finger. (Cringe!) No one knows for certain how the term "funny bone" originated, but some believe it's because part of the nerve sits near the humerus (pronounced *humorous*) bone, which sounds like it should be amusing.

ANIMAL ANTICS

LOST DOG!

Blind in one eye, chewed up right ear, missing front leg.

Answers to the name of "Lucky."

—*old joke with many versions*

"LET'S GO TICKLE some rats!"

It may sound a little strange, but that notion led one brain scientist to some big ideas.

For years, neuroscientist Jaak Panksepp had studied how rats playfully wrestle and knock heads. But he could never figure out the squeaky chirps they made as they tossed and tumbled—sounds so high humans could hear them only through an ultrasonic detector. Could the rats be needling one another? Were they calling for help? Panksepp tested all sorts of theories, but none explained his observations.

Then one day, he tickled the animals on the belly. One after another, the rats chirped in a recognizable rhythm. What's more, they kicked their legs like babies being tickled. When the scientist took a break, the rats followed his fingers and acted as if they wanted more. In time, the animals began anticipating the tickles, he says. "After a couple of trials, we could just wave our fingers in front of their noses and they would chirp."

Was this the sound of rat *laughter*?

Based on a variety of experiments, Panksepp believes it's a primitive form of laughter. Studies show that people could laugh well before they could speak, he points out in the journal *Science*. "Indeed, neural circuits for laughter exist in the very ancient regions of the brain"—those centers that evolved in humans and primitive mammals millions of years ago and that allow us to experience basic feelings, such as pleasure.

Panksepp believes that human joy may be rooted in animal laughter, since animals played and laughed long before we did. Younger children (who have limited language skills) often laugh and scream while chasing each other, he notes. "The same behavior patterns are evident in the 'play panting' of young chimps as they mischievously chase, mouth, and tickle each other." Panksepp thinks that the verbal jokes and puns people enjoy may be more advanced ways of tapping into the same playful, primitive parts of our brains. "As we learn to 'rib'

FOR BEST RESULTS TICKLE HERE:

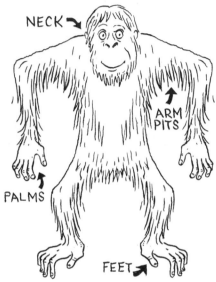

NECK

ARM PITS

PALMS

FEET

each other with words as opposed to rough-and-tumble horse-play," he says, the newly evolved, thinking parts of our brains may be connecting with the older, instinctual areas that help us to experience pleasure.

Rats and chimps aren't the only animals that make laughlike sounds. A British study found that gorillas, bonobos, and orangutans also pant sounds of delight when tickled on their necks, feet, palms, and armpits. The animal "laughs" communicate to others that they're playing and not fighting, theorizes laughter expert Robert Provine. He also links the *ah-ah-ah* sounds of a chimp's panting to the *ha-ha-ha* sounds of a person laughing. The difference lies in the ape's inability to control its breath in the same way as humans, he says.

It's not clear whether animals have a sense of humor as we know it, but they do appear to share the ability to have fun and express pleasure. Cats purr when content; dogs wag their tails when happy; and elephants trumpet and flap their ears when excited. Some animals even find ways to create their own good times. Hooded crows in Russia, for example, have been known to slide down the onion domes of the Kremlin again and again for no apparent reason other than to amuse themselves.

Animal Antics

"It's time to accept that animals have a wide range of emotions," says Panksepp, who currently serves as chairman of Animal Well-Being Science at Washington State University's College of Veterinary Medicine. The evidence now is overwhelming. "Although some still regard laughter as a uniquely human trait . . . the joke's on them."

✤ "I'm Going to Get You!" ✤

"Stop . . . stop . . . stop . . . I can't stand it!"

Tickling may be one of the oldest ways to make someone laugh, says researcher Robert Provine. It's a highly social interaction between a "tickler" and a "ticklee" that usually occurs with family and friends. In a survey of people ages eight to eighty-six, most said they tickled "to show affection" and that they enjoyed being tickled—despite the shrieks and squirms to escape.

But being tickled doesn't always feel like much fun—especially if it's taken to extremes. In fact, the ancient Romans tortured people by tickling them.

Scientists say we're in panic mode when we're being tickled. Our brain is trying to figure out when the next tickle "attack" will come. It's a natural defense mechanism that most likely came about as a way to alert us when unwelcome creatures wandered onto our skin. Imagine how you'd react if a spider was crawling up the back of your neck. Now think what it feels like when someone's about to tickle you. Your muscles tighten and your body prepares to defend itself, because you're not sure what to expect.

GOOCHY GOOCHY GOO!

YOU CAN'T FOOL ME!

This is one reason we can't tickle ourselves. The brain knows what we're about to do, so it barely reacts. "When you try to tickle yourself, the cerebellum [which is responsible for movement] predicts the sensation," explains British researcher Sarah-Jayne Blakemore. "This prediction is used to cancel the response of other brain areas to the tickle." In other words: no surprise, no tickle.

SNICKERS TO SNORTS

You sound a little hoarse.

Yeah, I feel a colt coming on.

—Pun of the Day Web site

LISTEN CLOSELY THE next time you're in a crowd. You may hear bird chirps, pig snorts, or frog croaks. Echoes of nature? Maybe. But more than likely they're the odd, sometimes animal-like noises people make when laughing. While we tend to classify laughs as hearty *ha-ha-ha*s, giggly *tee-hee-hee*s, or creepy *heh-heh-heh*s, they actually come in a variety of shapes and sizes—including a few that resemble chimpanzees panting.

"People have a rich repertoire of laugh sounds," says psychologist JoAnne Bachorowski of Vanderbilt University, a vocal communications researcher who has collected more than 30,000 laughs. These sounds vary in length and complexity—some wildly pitching up and down—but can be grouped into three broad categories:

1. **Songlike** laughs that are "voiced" and vibrate the vocal cords, giving them a vowel-like quality, such as *ha-ha-ha*

2. **Snortlike** laughs that project sounds primarily through the nose

3. **Gruntlike** laughs that project sounds primarily through the mouth, as in a pant or cackle

Songlike laughs have a catchy rhythm that is most apt to "grab a listener's attention or to make them feel good," says Bachorowski. "They're very acoustically pleasing." About half of women's laughs and a third of men's laughs are songlike. The rest fall into the snort- or gruntlike groupings and generally either annoy people or draw no particular reaction. Many laughs combine features from several categories. Some laughs, for example, start out with a wheezing sound called a "glottal whistle" before expanding to a songlike laugh. Since the wheeze always occurs at the beginning of a laugh, researchers think it's a way of grabbing people's attention and saying, "Hey, look at me, I'm about to laugh."

Much like the smile, says Bachorowski, laughter is often a way of making others feel happy so that they act more positively toward us. The blissful sounds can endear you to everyone from family and friends to strangers and authority figures. That includes teachers. Now isn't that music to your ears?

✵ Science with a Smile ✵

Do dog fleas jump higher than cat fleas?

Will a cow with a name make more milk?

Why don't pregnant women tip over?

Life's questions can be funny—and each year the Ig Nobel Prizes honor researchers who ask some of the funniest. The awards are parodies of the prestigious Nobel Prizes, which are presented each year for outstanding work in fields ranging from physics to literature. The spoof honors are given in comparable categories, along with a few others, such as mathematics and veterinary medicine.

"The Ig Nobel Prizes honor achievements that first make people laugh, and then make them think," say sponsors of the award, an organization called Improbable Research. They're "intended to celebrate the unusual, honor the imaginative—and spur people's interest in science, medicine, and technology." Among the winners are people who have examined panda poop, knuckle-cracking, and the side effects of sword-swallowing. (Sore throat?)

And, for the record—dog fleas jump higher than cat fleas.

LAUGH TRACKS

LAUGHTER IN A CAN?

Sometimes that's just what you need to get the giggles going. Laugh tracks—or canned chuckles—are prerecorded audience laughs played back during some television shows to punctuate funny moments. The idea is to trigger similar reactions from viewers, so they'll enjoy the program and tune in again.

"If you hear people laughing, you feel like laughing, too," says Robert Thompson, director of the Bleier Center for Television and Popular Culture at Syracuse University. "If nobody's laughing, it seems like what just happened wasn't funny." Laugh tracks can also make people feel like they're part of a larger community. "Millions of people can be watching the same show," says Thompson, "but they're watching one at a time. The laugh track links those people together to some extent. It stands in for all those other people you're watching the show with, but who just don't happen to be in the same room."

Laugh Tracks

Television laugh tracks debuted in 1950—in part to help with comic timing. "TV comedy was based in the traditions of radio and the vaudeville stage," says Thompson, and it followed a specific rhythm: one person set up a joke, another delivered the punch line, and then came a natural pause so the audience could let the fun sink in and laugh. Without an audience— or something resembling it— comedy scenes often fell flat.

Enter the laugh track, which not only energized early shows but enabled producers to shoot scenes outside the studio. At first, the canned laughs all sounded the same. But in the mid-1950s, Charlie Douglass introduced the "Laff Box"—an organlike instrument that played a variety of laughs at different volumes. With the press of a key, the sound engineer could instantly deliver everything from big belly laughs to silly snickers. Soon producers everywhere were calling on Charlie and his laugh machine to spice up their shows.

"A lot of the laugh tracks used in the beginning came from the *I Love Lucy* show," says Thompson. Unlike most television programs at the time, *Lucy* was filmed in front of a live studio audience, much like a play. It also featured plenty of physical comedy, which allowed for long, uninterrupted stretches of laughter.

Through the years, laugh tracks grew more sophisticated. "A good laugh track is one that's completely transparent—one that people simply don't pay attention to and aren't thinking about consciously," Thompson says. "My favorite example is *The Love Boat* [a romance comedy that ran in the 1970s and '80s and was set on a cruise ship floating in the middle of the ocean]. The big question was: Where in the world were these people laughing from?"

Today most shows have scaled back on laugh tracks, partly in response to critics who believe they offend people by telling them when to react. Laughs nowadays tend to be more subdued, says television historian Ben Glenn II. "You no longer hear unbridled belly laughs and guffaws." A few shows skip the laughs altogether—canned or otherwise. *The Office*, for example, relies on deadpan humor that's delivered matter-of-factly. Creators of the show trust that viewers will pick up on the absurdities and chuckle along when a situation strikes them as funny.

✹ Jest Texting ✹

Want to share a few virtual laughs? Check out the messaging lingo below and hit send!

BWL: Bursting with Laughter

CSL: Can't Stop Laughing

GOL: Giggling out Loud

HHOJ: HA HA Only Joking

JUADLAM: Jumping Up and Down Like a Monkey

LMHO: Laughing My Head Off

LSHMBH: Laughing So Hard My Belly Hurts

ROTFL: Rolling on the Floor Laughing

SFETE: Smiling from Ear to Ear

STAND AND DELIVER: COMEDY 101

Q: What do you call a dinosaur that's scared to tell a joke?

A: A nervous rex

—*common riddle with many variations*

THINK YOU'RE FUNNY . . . even just a little bit?

Then express yourself! You may want to be a comedian and tell jokes on stage, but that's not the only way to make people laugh. You can perform funny skits and songs, write silly stories and greeting cards, or draw comic strips and cartoons. You may even want to polish your humor skills to help make new friends or keep bullies at bay.

It's up to you to discover your talent, says top comedian and comedy coach Judy Carter. "You're as funny as you think you are." It also helps to look at the world a little differently, says Carter the author of a popular how-to book called *The Comedy Bible*. People who are funny notice weird things—like an uncle who picks his ears with his pinky or a dog that scoots along the carpet to scratch its butt. Little details rarely slip by them, she says. They spot the "turkey sandwitch" typo on

the lunch menu and the doughnuts in the gym teacher's locker. Comic personalities also tend to exaggerate and tell tall tales—the taller the better.

Comedian Jay Leno earned his first solo laughs while in class discussing Robin Hood.

"Can anyone tell us something about Robin's sidekick Friar Tuck?" the teacher asked.

"Friar Tuck was killed by the Sheriff of Nottingham by being boiled in oil," answered young Jay. "Do you know why they boiled him in oil?"

"No, why?" said his teacher.

"Because he was a friar.

"Get it? Boiled in oil because he was a fry-er."

Leno proudly recounts this story in his book *How to Be the Funniest Kid in the Whole Wide World (or Just in Your Class)*. At the time, the budding star didn't know (or care) *if* or *how* Friar Tuck was killed—he just wanted to make people laugh.

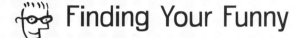 ## Finding Your Funny

Ask most comics where they get their ideas, and they typically point to family and friends, news reports, and day-to-day situations. In other words, everywhere. "I draw my material from real-life experiences," says comedian Mark Gonzalez of San Diego, who's the middle child in a family of five. "I look back at all the things that happened to me growing up and realize they happen to everyone else—just in another house." For example:

 My sister used to tell me I was adopted, because I didn't look like her or my brother.

So I asked my mother if I was adopted, and she told me no.

"You were an accident like everyone else."

 HA HA HA

What makes comedians such as Mark successful?

A little extra time and attention. People who turn their musings into funny material—jokes, stories, plays, and cartoons—take note of their ideas and write them down, says Judy Carter. One way the comedy coach recommends building this important habit is to spend the first

WHAT'S SO FUNNY?

ten minutes of each day capturing funny ideas in a notebook. Let your imagination flow, she tells students. Jot down odd thoughts, strange dreams, and events that strike you as funny. Draw silly pictures. If you have ideas for different types of comedy, divide your notebook into sections: one for jokes, another for cartoons, and maybe another for clever comebacks. A punch line can be a more effective weapon than a punch, she reminds us. Playwright Oscar Wilde knew this. Once after

APPLICATION.

RESULT.

APPLICATION.

RESULT.

one of his plays was performed, someone tossed a stinky cabbage at him. "Thank you, my dear fellow," he reportedly replied. "Every time I smell it, I shall be reminded of you."

No matter how many ideas you come up with, some will be funnier than others. In fact, most ideas probably won't be workable, says Carter. But this gives you a place to start. "Salespeople know that in order to have a sale, you have to make a lot of calls. Standup [comedy] is like that. The more jokes you write, the more chance you have of something working." When you dig up a few nuggets, put them in a separate file on cards, in a shoebox, or on the computer. The more ideas you collect, the more chance you'll have of discovering great material.

Why did the elephant cross the road? To meet with the chicken . . . To move his trunk . . . To trumpet on the corner . . . ? Keep playing until you like what you read.

Joking Around

Jokes take many forms, but they all include two important parts: the setup and the punch line. The *setup* usually poses a question or gives information that builds anticipation for the response. The *punch line* is the unexpected, funny response to the setup.

Setup: A man walks into a restaurant and asks the waiter, "Do you serve crabs?"

Punch line: "Of course," says the waiter. "We serve everyone!"

When writing your joke, adjust the rhythm of the words. Shorten it wherever you can—less is more. The fewer words you use to get to the punch line, the better. This also makes the joke easier to remember. Another great tip is to follow the "rule of threes." Use the first two lines in your joke to set up a pattern of expectation and then surprise listeners with a playful punch line.

A man calls the fire department and yells, "Help, help! My house is on fire!

The operator says, "Calm down. How do we get there?"

The man replies, "Don't you have those big red trucks anymore?"

Once you're happy with your joke, practice it out loud to help you tell it in the funniest way possible. Timing is everything. Many comedians pause briefly after the setup. This helps build suspense for the punch line.

Watching and listening to professionals telling jokes will also give you a sense of which words to emphasize and how you might tweak your approach. Go ahead and imitate your favorite comedians at first, advises Yakov Smirnoff. Retelling jokes and stories can help you build your confidence. (Just don't take credit for someone else's work!) Eventually, you'll develop your own "voice" and style.

When you're finally ready to test a joke with friends, tell it with confidence! Don't announce how funny it is beforehand, let them decide. If it's a success and they laugh, keep up the great work. If they're not too crazy about it, no big deal. Move on—not every joke's going to be a hit, says Smirnoff, especially in the beginning.

If somebody heckles you, "deal with it quickly," recommends Leno. You may want to have a comeback ready, adds Carter—a snappy retort such as, "Thank you for sharing," or "Oh, stop it Mom!"

In any case, don't give up! Keep working at it, urges comedian and international speaker Darren LaCroix, who acknowledges he wasn't a very funny kid. "In fact, the first time my brother ever laughed at me was when I told him I was going to be a comedian. . . . OUCH!" In times like these, he says, it's important to "be an OUCH master."

Don't be afraid to get back up after a fall. "It's the step after the OUCH that's so important." It's the one that we learn the most from, he says. "It's the step that moves you forward." Who knows? Maybe someday into a career in comedy!

✿ DID YOU KNOW? ✿

World Laughter Day is celebrated each year on the first Sunday in May. Created by Dr. Madan Kataria of India in 1998, its goal is to promote world peace through laughter. Dr. Kataria is also the founder of Laughter Yoga, a form of exercise where people pretend to laugh until it becomes real, so that they can reap laughter's healthful benefits.

Aphrilophobia is the fear of April Fools' Day. People with this social phobia panic at the thought of being tricked and embarrassed by others.

The Mark Twain Prize for American Humor, named in honor of the nineteenth-century author known for his keen wit and humorous stories, is a prestigious award given annually to a person who has contributed greatly to American humor. Recipients include Whoopi Goldberg, Steve Martin, and Bill Cosby.

Saint-Louis-du-Ha! Ha! is a small town in Quebec, Canada. Its unusual name comes from an old French word, *le haha*, which means an impasse or dead end. When early explorers paddled canoes across Lake Témiscouata, they would hit a patch of land they called the *haha*. Eventually, settlers started communities at the site—including Saint-Louis-du-[of the]-Haha. At first, the name didn't include exclamation points, but mapmakers reportedly couldn't resist adding them along the way.

The Laughing Kookaburra (KUK-uh-bur-uh), a bird native to Australia, has an unusually loud territorial call that mimics the sounds of laughter. It starts with a soft chuckle, revs up to several lively *hoo-hoo-hoo-hoo, ha-ha-ha-ha, hoo-hoo-hoo-hoos*, and ends with another chuckle.

✿ MORE GOOD HUMOR! ✿

TO LEARN MORE about humor, check out these resources.

Publications

Becker, Helaine, illustrated by Claudia Davila. *Funny Business: Clowning Around, Practical Jokes, Cool Comedy, Cartooning, and More . . .* Toronto: Maple Tree Press, 2005.

Brewer, Paul. *You Must Be Joking!* Peterborough, N.H.: Cricket Books, 2003.

Leno, Jay. *How to Be the Funniest Kid in the Whole Wide World (or Just in Your Class)*. New York: Simon & Schuster Books for Young Readers, 2005.

Marcus, Leonard S., editor. *Funny Business: Conversations with Writers of Comedy*. Cambridge, Mass.: Candlewick Press, 2009.

Web Sites

Celebrating World Laughter Day: www.worldlaughterday.org.

Exploratorium: Mind Lecture Series: The Science of Laughter: www.exploratorium.edu/mind/ponder/videos.php.

Improbable Research: http://improbable.com.

Laugh Sounds: www.psy.vanderbilt.edu/faculty/bachorowski/laugh.htm.

The Museum of Hoaxes: www.museumofhoaxes.com.

Pun of the Day: www.punoftheday.com..

✿ SOURCE NOTES ✿

What's Soooooo Funny?

"We're all born . . ." "It's like a . . ." and "moment of discovery": Exploratorium Museum, "The Science of Laughter."

Humor has also been . . . : Sultanoff, "What Is Humor?"

You know, like the . . . : Sennett, *101 Stunts for Principals to Inspire Student Achievement*.

"When you experience . . .": Sultanoff interview

"Humor tends to reduce . . .": Sultanoff, "What Is Humor?"

Humor can even . . . : Sultanoff interview.

"it's not the situations . . . ": Sultanoff, "What Is Humor?"

"Sometimes, we'll laugh . . .": Martin interview.

"I'm so afraid of heights . . .": Jackson interview.

"It probably evolved . . .": Martin interview

"The superiority theory . . ." and Many jokes . . . : Wiseman, LaughLab.

"Did you hear . . .": Wiseman, *Quirkology*.

"where they could get hold . . .": Boese, "The Top 100 April Fool's Day Hoaxes of All Time."

"The doctor gives . . .": The British Association for the Advancement of Science, *LaughLab*.

"exaggeration humor": Sultanoff, interview.

"no real harm . . .": Ramachandran, *A Brief Tour of Human Conscious5ness*.

A third . . . : Sultanoff, "What Is Humor?"

"A man's at home . . .": Wali Collins, e-mail interview.

Different Strokes

"They laugh loudest . . ." and "When somebody slips . . .": Sultanoff interview.

Often they'll tease . . . : Martin, *The Psychology of Humor*.

Many times . . . : Sultanoff interview.

"for the purpose of . . ." "group solidarity" . . . When shown videotapes . . . and Experts think . . . : Martin, *The Psychology of Humor*.

"Humor is basically . . ." and "It's hilarious . . .": McGhee, "Head, Shoulders, Knees and . . . Peanut Butter."

"riddle disease": McGhee, "Children's Riddles."

"*Did you hear* . . . :" Black, Pun of the Day Web site.

One study, noted . . . Most day-to-day . . . and Studies show that . . . : Martin, *The Psychology of Humor*.

Like many around the world . . . : Evans, "But Will They Laugh in Minsk?"

"In Britain and Australia . . .": Davis, interview.

"An Alsatian dog went . . .": Wiseman, LaughLab.

warai no ba . . . and "It's a time . . .": Davis interview.

"Local Chinese people . . ." and "It's a cultural thing": Gong interview.

"Thus a 'humor' . . . in public in the United States": Martin, *The Psychology of Humor*.

Humor Styles

How we use humor . . . : Martin, interview.

four main types of humor . . . : Identified by Martin in *The Psychology of Humor* as affiliative, self-enhancing, aggressive, and self-defeating; renamed bonding, laugh-at-life, put-down, and laugh-at-me in Dobson, "What's Your Humor Style?"

"I was a funny kid . . .": Smirnoff interview.

"exaggeration humor": Sultanoff interview.

Laughing Matters

"hosts an *A'wee Chi'deedloh* . . .": Goodwin-Boyd, "First Laugh, Navajo."

Even infants . . . : Martin, *The Psychology of Humor*.

"Laughter's about relationships . . . honest signals": Provine, "The Science of Laughter."

Take the strange case . . . : The Infinite Mind, "Laughter."

"The incubation period . . .": Rankin, "An Epidemic of Laughing in the Bukoba District of Tanganyika."

While the case . . . : Provine, *Laughter: A Scientific Investigation*.

Source Notes

Provine played recorded laughs . . . : Provine, "The Science of Laughter."

researchers in England . . . : Thompson, "Laughter Really Is Contagious, Study Finds."

"auditory laugh detector . . ." and "Once triggered . . .": Provine, "The Science of Laughter."

"a robust contagious laughter": Fried, "Electric Current Stimulates Laughter."

All in Your Head: Elkan, "The Comedy Circuit."

"the logic by which . . . than we might think": quoted in Elkan, "The Comedy Circuit."

"internal jogging": Cousins, *Head First*.

Experts say holding back . . . : Berk, "The Active Ingredient in Humor."

Animal Antics

"Let's go tickle . . . ": Radiolab, "Laughter."

"After a couple . . . rough-and-tumble horse-play": Panksepp, "Beyond a Joke."

A British study . . . : Handwerk, "Apes Laugh, Tickle Study Finds."

The animal "laughs" . . . : Provine, *Laughter: A Scientific Investigation*.

Hooded crows in Russia . . . : Shuker, *The Hidden Power of Animals*.

"It's time to accept . . .": Panksepp, e-mail correspondence.

"Although some . . .": Panksepp, "Beyond a Joke."

Tickling may be . . . "to show affection": Provine, *Laughter: A Scientific Investigation*.

Scientists say we're . . . : Edmonds, "Why Can't You Tickle Yourself?"

"When you try . . . ": Blakemore, "Why Can't You Tickle Yourself?"

Snickers to Snorts

"People have a rich . . . ": As quoted in Harris, "Laughter's Influence."

"grab a listener's attention . . . ": The Infinite Mind, "Laughter."

"The Ig Nobel Prizes . . .": Improbable Research, "Winners of the Ig Nobel Prize."

Laugh Tracks

"If you hear . . . the vaudeville stage": Thompson, interview.

But in the . . . : Bennett, "Don't Make Me Laugh."

"A lot of . . ." "A good laugh . . ." and "My favorite example . . .": Thompson, interview.

"You no longer hear . . .": Sacks, "Canned Laughter."

Stand and Deliver: Comedy 101

"You're as funny . . .": Carter, *The Comedy Bible*.

"Can anyone tell . . . he was a fry-er": Leno, *How to Be the Funniest Kid in the Whole Wide World*.

"I draw my . . . else": Gonzalez, e-mail interview.

A little extra . . . : Carter, *The Comedy Bible*.

"Thank you, my dear . . .": Grothe, *Viva la Repartee*.

"Sales people know . . .": Carter, e-mail interview.

"A man walks into . . .": Popik, "Do You Serve Crabs Here?"

"A man calls . . .": The British Association for the Advancement of Science 2002, *LaughLab*.

Go ahead and imitate . . . : Smirnoff interview.

"deal with it quickly": Leno, *How to Be the Funniest Kid in the Whole Wide World*.

"Thank you for sharing . . .": Carter, e-mail correspondence.

Keep working at it . . . : LaCroix interview.

"In fact, the first time . . ." and "be an OUCH master . . .": LaCroix, "Ouch!"

Did You Know?

Aphrilophobia is the fear . . . : English Word Information.

The Mark Twain prize . . . : The Kennedy Center.

Saint-Louis-du-Ha! Ha!: Saint-Louis-du-Ha! Ha! Web site and Jeffries, "The Joy of Exclamation Marks!"

✵ BIBLIOGRAPHY ✵

Bennett, Drake. "Don't Make Me Laugh." Slate.com/ September 19, 2007.

Berk, Ronald A. "The Active Ingredient in Humor: Psychophysiological Benefits and Risks for Older Adults." *Educational Gerontology*, 2001.

Black, John. E-mail interview, May 14, 2010.

Black, John. Pun of the Day Web site: www.punoftheday.com

Blakemore, Sarah-Jayne, Daniel Wolpert, and Chris Frith. "Why Can't You Tickle Yourself?" *NeuroReport*, August 2000.

Boese, Alex. "The Top 100 April Fool's Day Hoaxes of All Time." The Museum of Hoaxes: www.museum ofhoaxes.com.

The British Association for the Advancement of Science 2002. *LaughLab*. London: Arrow Books Limited, 2002.

Carter, Judy. *The Comedy Bible*. New York: Fireside, 2001.

Carter, Judy. E-mail interview. March 6, 2009.

Collins, Wali. E-mail interview, February 13, 2010.

Cousins, Norman. *Head First*. New York: Penguin, 1990

Dobson, Louise. "What's Your Humor Style?" *Psychology Today*, August 2006.

Edmonds, Molly. "Why Can't You Tickle Yourself?" Discovery Health: http://health.howstuffworks.com/ mental-health/human-nature/other-emotions/question511.htm.

Elkan, Daniel. "The Comedy Circuit: When Your Brain Gets the Joke." *New Scientist*, January 30, 2010.

English-Word Information. Senior Scribe Publications: www.wordinfo.info.

Evans, Rory. "But Will They Laugh in Minsk?" *Reader's Digest*, September 2009.

Exploratorium Museum. "The Science of Laughter." Interview with Dr. William Fry. November 10, 2007: http://www.exploratorium.edu/media/index.php?cmd=browse&project=58&program= 00000543&type=webcast.

Fried, Itzhak, et al. "Electric Current Stimulates Laughter." *Nature*, February 12, 1998.

Gong, Jami. E-mail interview, March 26, 2009. Author interview, February 11, 2010.

Gonzalez, Mark. E-mail interview, September 21, 2009.

Goodwin-Boyd, Putnam. "First Laugh, Navajo." Wondertime: http://wondertime.go.com/learning/article/ navajo-baby-laugh.html.

Bibliography

Grothe, Mardy. *Viva la Repartee: Clever Comebacks and Witty Retorts from History's Great Wits and Wordsmiths*. New York: Collins, 2005.

Handwerk, Brian. "Apes Laugh, Tickle Study Finds." *National Geographic News*, June 4, 2009.

Harris, Lew. "Laughter's Influence," *Exploration*, January 9, 2001.

Improbable Research. "Winners of the Ig Nobel Prize": http://improbable.com/ig/winners/.

The Infinite Mind. "Humor." Week of August 28, 2007: http://www.lcmedia.com/mind494.htm.

The Infinite Mind. "Laughter." Week of March 20, 2007: http://www.lcmedia.com/mind471.htm.

Jackson, Charles. Author interview, July 16, 2010.

Jeffries, Stuart. "The Joy of Exclamation Marks!" *The Guardian*, April 29, 2009.

The Kennedy Center. Mark Twain Prize for American Humor: www.kennedy-center.org/programs/specialevents/marktwain.

LaCroix, Darren. Author interview, October 1, 2009.

LaCroix, Darren. "Ouch!" Toastmasters International World Championship of Public Speaking first-place speech, 2001: http://www.angelfire.com/az2/D3tmLeadership3/DarrenLaCroix_Speech.html

Leno, Jay. *How to Be the Funniest Kid in the Whole Wide World (or Just in Your Class)*. New York: Simon & Schuster Books for Young Readers, 2005.

Martin, Rod A. Author interview, September 28, 2009.

Martin, Rod A. *The Psychology of Humor*. London: Elsevier Academic Press, 2007.

McGhee, Paul E. "Children's Riddles: The First Sign of an Adult Sense of Humor." The Laughter Remedy: http://www.laughterremedy.com/article_pdfs/Children's%20Riddles.pdf.

McGhee, Paul E., "Head, Shoulders, Knees and . . . Peanut Butter: What Makes Young Children Laugh?" The Laughter Remedy: http://www.laughterremedy.com/article_pdfs/Developmental%20changes.pdf.

NetLingo. "Acronyms & Text Message": http://www.netlingo.com/category/acronyms.php.

Panksepp, Jaak. "Beyond a Joke: From Animal Laughter to Human Joy?" *Science Magazine*, April 1, 2005.

Panksepp, Jaak. E-mail correspondence, March 5, 2010.

Popik, Barry. "Do You Serve Crabs Here?" The Big Apple, March 19, 2009: http://www.barrypopik.com/index.php/new_york_city/entry/do_you_serve_crabs_here_joke/.

Provine, Robert. "A Big Mystery: Why Do We Laugh?" MSNBC.com, May 27, 1999: http://www.msnbc.msn.com/id/3077386/.

Provine, Robert R. *Laughter: A Scientific Investigation*, New York: Viking, 2000.

Bibliography

Provine, Robert R. "The Science of Laughter." *Psychology Today*, November/December 2000.

Radiolab. "Laughter." WNYC, February 22, 2008: http://www.wnyc.org/shows/radiolab/episodes/2008/02/22.

Ramachandran, V. S. *A Brief Tour of Human Consciou5ness*, New York: Pi Press, 2004.

Rankin, A. M., and P. J. Philip. "An Epidemic of Laughing in the Bukoba District of Tanganyika." *Central African Journal of Medicine*, May 1963. Reproduced in the Radio Lab in Tanzania blog, May 31, 2007: http://rltz.blogspot.com/2007/05/from-central-african-medical-journal.html.

Sacks, Mike. "Canned Laughter: A History Reconstructed: An Interview with Ben Glenn II, Television Historian: And Here's the Kicker": www.andheresthekicker.com/ex_ben_glenn.php.

Saint-Louis-du-Ha! Ha! Web site: www.saintlouisduhaha.com.

Seaward, Brian Luke. *Managing Stress: Principles and Strategies for Health and Well-Being*, Fifth Edition. Boston: Jones and Bartlett Publishers, 2006.

Sennett, Frank. *101 Stunts for Principals to Inspire Student Achievement.* Thousand Oaks, Calif.: Corwin Press, 2004.

Shuker, Karl P. N. *The Hidden Power of Animals.* Pleasantville, N.Y.: Reader's Digest, 2001.

Smirnoff, Yakov. Author interview, October 21, 2009.

Sultanoff, Steven M. Author interview, February 25, 2010.

Sultanoff, Steven M. Humor Matters Web site: www.humormatters.com.

Sultanoff, Steven M. "What Is Humor?" Association for Applied and Therapeutic Humor. Humor Resources: http://www.aath.org/articles/art_sultanoff01.html.

Thompson, Andrea. "Laughter Really Is Contagious, Study Finds." *LiveScience*, December 12, 2006.

Thompson, Robert J. Author interview, September 18, 2009.

Wiseman, Richard. LaughLab.co.uk.

Wiseman, Richard. *Quirkology: How We Discover the Big Truths in Small Things*. New York: Basic Books, 2007.

❈ INDEX ❈

Index